Air Fryer Oven Recipe Guide

The Best Quick and Easy Recipes to Grill, Fry, Bake, and Toast for Everyday Cooking

Table of Contents

INTRODUCTION: **8**

CHAPTER 1: UNTOLD BENEFITS OF AN AIR FRYER YOU MAY NOT KNOW **10**

CHAPTER 2: AIR FRYER OVEN TIPS & TRICKS AND ITS FUNCTION KEYS **12**

CHECK FOOD DURING COOKING 12

CLEANING THE AIR FRYER..13

FUNCTION KEYS 13

CHAPTER 3: BREAKFAST...**16**

1.   AVOCADO FLAUTAS 16

2.   CHEESE SANDWICHES 19

3.   SAUSAGE CHEESE WRAPS 21

4.   CHICKEN OMELET 22

5.   SAUSAGE BURRITOS 24

6.   SAUSAGE PATTIES 26

CHAPTER 4: MAINS **28**

7.   ROSEMARY GRILLED CHICKEN 28

8.   CURRIED COCONUT CHICKEN 30

9.   TURKEY AND QUINOA STUFFED PEPPERS 32

CHAPTER 5: SIDES **34**

10.   BAKED VEGETABLES 34

11.   CHEESE HERB ZUCCHINI...36

12.   HEALTHY SPINACH MUFFINS..38

CHAPTER 6: SEAFOOD...**40**

13.   SALMON DILL PATTIES..40

14.   SPICY SHRIMP 42

15. AIR FRIED WHITE FISH FILLET 43

16. MUSTARD-CRUSTED SOLE FILLETS 45

17. SOLE AND CAULIFLOWER FRITTERS 47

18. PARMESAN-CRUSTED SALMON PATTIES 49

CHAPTER 7: POULTRY **52**

19. CRISP CHICKEN W/ MUSTARD VINAIGRETTE 52

20. CHICKEN WITH OREGANO-ORANGE CHIMICHURRI & ARUGULA SALAD 55

21. STIR-FRIED CHICKEN WITH WATER CHESTNUTS 57

22. PERFECTLY FRIED CHICKEN ROAST SERVED WITH FRUIT COMPOTE 59

23. LEMON PEPPER CHICKEN LEGS 61

CHAPTER 8: MEAT **62**

24. HOT FLANK STEAKS WITH ROASTED PEANUTS 62

25. AUTHENTIC WIENER BEEF SCHNITZEL 64

26. DREAMY BEEF STEAK WITH RICE, BROCCOLI AND GREEN BEANS 65

27. MUSTARD PORK CHOPS WITH LEMON ZEST 67

28. HERBED BEEF ROAST 69

29. ROAST PORK BELLY WITH CUMIN 70

30. SUNDAY NIGHT GARLIC BEEF SCHNITZEL 72

CHAPTER 9: VEGETABLES **74**

31. GARLICKY CAULIFLOWER FLORETS 74

32. FLAVORS GREEN BEANS 76

33. POTATO CASSEROLE 78

34. ZUCCHINI EGG BAKE 80

35. BALSAMIC BAKED MUSHROOMS 82

CHAPTER 10: SOUP **84**

36. BARLEY BEEF SOUP 84

37. ITALIAN VEGETABLE SOUP 86

CHAPTER 11: SNACKS **88**

38. BUFFALO QUESADILLAS 88

39. CRISPY SAUSAGE BITES 90

40. PUFFED ASPARAGUS SPEARS 92

41. RABAS IS A HOT AIR FRYER 94

CHAPTER 12: DESSERTS **96**

42. AIR FRIED BUTTER CAKE 96

43. CHOCOLATE CHIP COOKIES.....................................98

44. AIR FRYER S'MORES 101

45. DOUBLE-GLAZED CINNAMON BISCUIT BITES................103

46. APPLE CIDER DONUTS 105

47. BREAD DOUGH AND AMARETTO DESSERT................109

48. TASTY BANANA CAKE 111

49. PUMPKIN PIE..112

CHAPTER 13: SPECIAL RECIPE **114**

50. HONEY DUCK BREASTS 114

CONCLUSION **116**

Introduction:

An air fryer is a present-day kitchen appliance that cooks food by circulating hot air instead of oil. It offers a light version of foods that are traditionally cooked in the fryer. As a result, most unhealthy foods such as French fries, fried chicken, and onion rings are cooked without oil or up to 80% less fat than conventional cooking methods. An air fryer provides healthier foods and fried foods, allowing you to get rid of the calories gained by eating fried foods while providing you with a crispy texture, texture, and quality. This appliance operates by circulating hot air (up to 400 ° F) evenly and quickly around food ingredients housed indoors. The variety of cooking options makes it easy to prepare any type of food at any time of the day.

Why Use It

Low-Fat Meals: Unarguably, the most fundamental advantage of the air fryer is its use of hot-air course to cook food ingredients from all points, accordingly taking out the need for oil use. That makes it workable for people on a low-fat eating regimen to serenely get ready for magnificently good meals. More beneficial Foods& Environment: Air fryers are intended to work without stuffing oils and deliver more good foods with up to 80 percent less fat. That makes it simpler to shed pounds because you can eat your seared dishes while saving calories and immersed fat. Making that change to a more useful life is progressively feasible by utilizing this appliance. Your house is also freed of the fragrance that accompanies deep singed foods that regularly remain around the climate even a few hours after deep searing.

Multipurpose Use: The air fryer empowers you to perform various tasks to set up numerous dishes immediately. You're across the board appliance that can flame broil, bake, fry, and meal those dishes you love! You never again need numerous machines for different occupations. It can do other employments separate appliances will do.

It can flame broil meat, cook veggies, and bake baked goods. It fills in as a compelling substitution for your broiler, deep fryer, and stovetop.

Simple Clean Up: The Air Fryer leaves no oil and, consequently, no wreckage. Clean-up time is pleasant since their oils spill to clean on dividers and floors, and no rejecting or scouring of the skillet. There is no need to invest in energy, guaranteeing that everything is immaculate. The Air fryer parts are made of a non-stick material that keeps food from adhering to surfaces, making it difficult to clean. These parts are anything but difficult to clean and keep up. They are removable and dishwasher-protected also.

Spare Valuable Time: People on tight timetables can utilize the air fryer's quickness to make delightful meals. For cases, you can make French fries in less than 15 minutes and bake a cake inside 25 minutes. Inside minutes as well, you can appreciate firm chicken fingers or brilliant fries. If you are consistently in a hurry, the air fryer is perfect for you because you will invest less energy in the kitchen. It empowers you to deal with your boisterous and occupied day by day life, making your day progressively sensible.

Air Fryer Oven Recipe Guide

CHAPTER 1:

Untold Benefits of an Air Fryer You May Not Know

Y ou may begin to wonder why you need to use an air fryer and those things that make it unique. Well, you are not alone on this. Many people have been in your shoes before as they wondered why the hype about air fryers. I used to think like that too, but now I know better! An air fryer has many untold benefits, and here are some of them.

Health wise, an air fryer is great because it helps you healthily prepare food. If you recall, too much oil is not suitable for your health, but when you deep-fry, you have no choice but to immerse the food in fat, and it absorbs most of the oil. That is why fried foods are not healthy because they soak up too much oil while in the preparation process. Unfortunately, you eventually consume this oil.

With the unique design that makes an air fryer so compact, you don't have to wait for so long to preheat because it is cut down to just two (2) or three (3) minutes! With this, you don't just save time; you save energy too. You don't need to worry about heating the whole kitchen in summer because you can preheat your air fryer, and the entire kitchen won't be heated up.

Why should you spend so much time cooking when you can get things done faster with an air fryer? Due to the intense heat created when using an air fryer, meals are cooked pretty quickly than in an oven, about 20% faster, saving energy. You probably don't have much time to spare while cooking, and the manufacturers of your air fryer know about this, designing the cooking device in a way that will help you save time.

10 | P a g .

The air fryer is safer and easier to use than deep-frying because this cooking appliance mostly has settings for your preferred temperature and time. With the scenes, all you have to do set your preferences, and that's all! You don't have to go through the stress of heating a pot containing oil on your stovetop or register temperature with a deep-frying thermometer.

What about the stress of continually checking the heat below to ensure that the temperature is stable? The emphasis is just too much. Since you are dealing with lots of oil that can become a danger when very hot and getting rid of the fat can be tiring, why not save yourself from this stress by using an air fryer?

I know that feeling and how irritating it can be when your kitchen is messed up after cooking. Keeping the kitchen clean and tidy at all times is a must, and with an air fryer, you can achieve this quickly. Unlike your conventional cooking method, an air fryer prevents food from splattering around because everything you are cooking with is kept in a sealed space. Not just that, you can easily clean and maintain the air fryer, and I will share some helpful tips to do so.

CHAPTER 2:

Air Fryer Oven Tips & Tricks and Its Function Keys

ir fryer Ovens are designed to be super easy to use. The air fryer does a great job of making food crispy because of the convection function. Here's a little tip to get you started:

Gather the ingredients for the recipe and prep them according to the instructions. When prepped, put the ingredients into the air fryer or in the basket, rack, or pans within the air fryer. Use parchment baking paper or a light mist of oil spray to prevent food from sticking.

Never crowd food in the air fryer or over-fill. Food that is sealed in the air fryer won't cook evenly and can be raw and under-cooked. If you're preparing for a crowd, you may have to cook more than one batch.

Setting the Temperature and Time

Check the recipe for the correct temperature and time setting. You can set manually; you can use the digital location for the weather and time needed for the recipe. Most air fryers also have preset functions that make it easy to set according to each recipe.

Check Food During Cooking

Many air fryer oven recipes require you to check the food while cooking to cooks evenly and don't over-cook. You will need to shake, flip, or toss the food to distribute it. Or for some recipes, you'll need to turn the food about halfway through when cooking so that it cooks and crisps all the way thoroughly

Cleaning The Air Fryer

Once the food is cooked, remove, and unplug the air fryer. Let it cool completely before cleaning. Follow the directions that come with the air fryer oven for proper cleaning. Never scrub or use abrasive cleaners when cleaning the fryer or the fryer accessories.

Using the Basket or Rack

Some air fryers use a round basket where foods are cooked, while other models will have layered racks that fit into a square cooking space, much like a small oven. Most of the recipes given in this cookbook can be used for both baskets and racks.

Keep an Eye on Timing

You'll find that air fryers cook at different temperatures depending on what model you have. It's essential to check on foods during the cooking process, so you don't over or undercook them. If you've cut back on quantities in some of the recipes, be sure to cut the cooking time down accordingly.

Remember, hints are just recommendations to guide you as you use your air fryer.

Using Oil Sprays

Most of the recipes use an oil spray. But if you desire, you can use any brand you want. Or make your own by merely putting olive oil into a small spray bottle. Use a small amount of fat and spray over the basket and trays to prevent food from sticking. Some of the recipes require you to stream the food with oil directly.

Function Keys

The following are the functions keys of an Air Fryer Oven:

Play/Pause Button

This Play/Pause button allows you to pause during the middle of the cooking so you can shake the air fryer basket or flip the food to ensure it cooks evenly.

-/+ Button /Minus or Plus Button

This button is used to change the time or temperature.

Keep Warm

This function keeps your food warm for 30 minutes.

Food Presets

This button gives you the ability to cook food without second-guessing. The time and temperature are already set, so new users find this setting useful.

Roast or Broil

You can roast or broil with this setting. When using a conventional oven, you need to brown the meat before roasting. You can skip this step when cooking with an air fryer.

Dehydrate

This setting cooks and dries food at a low temperature for a few hours. With this option, you can create your beef jerky or dried fruit.

CHAPTER 3:

BREAKFAST

1.   Avocado Flautas

Preparation Time: 10 minutes

Cooking Time: 24 minutes

Serving: 8

Ingredients:

- 1 tbsp. butter

- Eight eggs, beaten

- ½ tsp. Salt

- ¼ tsp. pepper

- 1 ½ tsp. cumin

- 1 tsp. chili powder

- Eight fajita-size tortillas

- 4 oz. cream cheese softened

- Eight slices of cooked bacon

- Avocado Crème:

- Two small avocados

- ½ cup sour cream

- One lime, juiced

- ½ tsp. Salt

- ¼ tsp. pepper

Directions:

1.   In a skillet, melt butter and stir in eggs, salt, cumin, pepper, and chili powder, then stir cook for 4 minutes. Spread all the tortillas and top them with cream cheese and bacon. Then divide the egg scramble on top and finally add cheese.

2.   Roll the tortillas to seal the filling inside. Place four rolls in the Air Fryer basket. Set the Air Fryer basket inside the Air

Fryer toaster oven and close the lid. Select the Air Fry mode at 400 degrees F temperature for 12 minutes.

3.   Cook the remaining tortilla rolls in the same manner. Meanwhile, blend avocado crème ingredients in a blender, then serve with warm flautas.

Nutrition:

Calories: 212   Protein: 17.3gCarbs: 14.6gFat: 11.8g

2.   Cheese Sandwiches

Preparation Time: 10 minutes

Cooking Time: 10 minutes

Serving: 2

Ingredients:

- One egg

- 3 tbsp. Half and half cream

- ¼ tsp. vanilla extract

- Two slices sourdough, white or multigrain bread

- 2½ oz. sliced Swiss cheese

- 2 oz. sliced deli ham

- 2 oz. cut deli turkey

- 1 tsp. butter, melted

- Powdered sugar

- Raspberry jam, for serving

Directions:

1.   Beat egg with half and half cream and vanilla extract in a bowl. Place one bread slice on the working surface and top it with ham and turkey slice and Swiss cheese.

2.	Place the other bread slice on top, then dip the sandwich in the egg mixture, then place it in a suitable baking tray lined with butter. Set the baking tray inside the Air Fryer toaster oven and close the lid.

3.	Select the Air Fry mode at 350 degrees F temperature for 10 minutes. Flip the sandwich and continue cooking for 8 minutes. Slice and serve.

Nutrition:

Calories: 412	Protein: 18.9gCarbs: 43.8gFat: 24.8g

3.   Sausage Cheese Wraps

Preparation Time: 10 minutes

Cooking Time: 10 minutes

Serving: 4

Ingredients:

- Eight sausages

- Two pieces American cheese, shredded

- 8-count refrigerated crescent roll dough

Directions:

1.   Roll out each crescent roll and top it with cheese and one sausage. Fold both the crescent sheet's top and bottom edges to cover the link and roll it around the sausage.

2.   Place four rolls in the Air Fryer basket and spray them with cooking oil. Set the Air Fryer basket inside the Air Fryer toaster oven and close the lid. Select the Air Fry mode at 380 degrees F temperature for 3 minutes.

3.   Cook the remaining rolls in the same manner. Serve fresh.

Nutrition:

Calories: 296   Protein: 34.2gCarbs: 17gFat: 22.1g

4.   Chicken Omelet

Preparation Time: 10 minutes

Cooking Time: 18 minutes

Serving: 4

Ingredients:

- Four eggs

- ½ cup chicken breast, cooked and diced

- 2 tbsp. Shredded cheese, divided

- ½ tsp. Salt divided

- ¼ tsp. Pepper divided

- ¼ tsp. Granulated garlic, divided

- ¼ tsp. onion powder, divided

Directions:

1.   Spray two ramekins with cooking oil and keep them aside. Crack two large eggs into each ramekin, and then add cheese and seasoning.

2.   Whisk well, and then add ¼ cup chicken. Place the ramekins in a baking tray.

3.   Set the baking tray inside the Air Fryer toaster oven and close the lid. Select the Bake mode at 330 degrees F temperature for 18 minutes. Serve warm.

Nutrition:

Calories: 322   Protein: 17.3gCarbs: 4.6gFat: 21.8g

5.   Sausage Burritos

Preparation Time: 10 minutes

Cooking Time: 10 minutes

Serving: 6

Ingredients:

- Six medium flour tortillas

- Six scrambled eggs

- ½ lb. ground sausage, browned

- ½ bell pepper, minced

- 1/3 cup bacon bits

- ½ cup shredded cheese

- Oil, for spraying

Directions:

1.   Mix eggs with cheese, bell pepper, bacon, and sausage in a bowl. Spread each tortilla on the working surface and top it with ½ cup egg filling.

2.   Roll the tortilla like a burrito, then place three burritos in the Air Fryer basket.

3.   Spray them with cooking oil. Set the Air Fryer basket inside the Air Fryer toaster oven and close the lid. Select

the Air Fry mode at 330 degrees F temperature for 5 minutes.

4.   Cook the remaining burritos in the same manner. Serve fresh.

Nutrition:

Calories: 197   Protein: 7.9gCarbs: 58.5gFat: 15.4g

6.   Sausage Patties

Preparation Time: 10 minutes

Cooking Time: 20 minutes

Serving: 4

Ingredients:

- 1.5 lbs. ground sausage

- 1 tsp. chili flakes

- 1 tsp. dried thyme

- 1 tsp. Onion powder

- ½ tsp. each paprika and cayenne

- Sea salt and black pepper, to taste

- 2 tsp. brown sugar

- 3 tsp. minced garlic

- 2 tsp. Tabasco

- Herbs for garnish

Directions:

1.   Toss sausage ground with all the spices, herbs, sugar, garlic, and Tabasco sauce in a bowl. Make 1.5-inch-thick and 3-inch round patties out of this mixture.

2.   Place the sausage patties in the Air Fryer basket. Set the Air Fryer basket inside the Air Fryer toaster oven and close the lid. Select the Air Fry mode at 370 degrees F temperature for 20 minutes.

3.   Flip the patties when cooked halfway through, and then continue cooking.

Nutrition:

Calories: 208   Protein: 24.3gCarbs: 9.5gFat: 10.7g

CHAPTER 4:

Mains

7.   Rosemary Grilled Chicken

Preparation Time: 10 minutes

Cooking time: 10 minutes

Servings: 4

Ingredients:

- One teaspoon sea salt

- One tablespoon fresh parsley, finely chopped

- One tablespoon fresh rosemary, finely chopped

- One tablespoon olive oil

- Five cloves garlic, minced

- Four pieces of 6-oz chicken breast, boneless and skinless

Directions:

1. In a shallow and large bowl, mix salt, parsley, rosemary, olive oil, and garlic. Place chicken breast and marinate in a bowl of herbs for at least an hour or more before grilling.

2. Grease grill grates and preheat grill to medium-high. Once hot, grill chicken for 4 to 5 minutes per side or until juices run a transparent and internal chicken temperature is 168oF.

Nutrition:

Calories 317, Total Fat 9g, Saturated Fat 2.2g, Total Carbs 1g, Net Carbs 0.8g, Protein 53g, Sugar: 0g, Fiber 0.2g, Sodium 709mg, Potassium 459mg

8.   Curried Coconut Chicken

Preparation Time: 10 minutes Cooking time: 40 minutes

Servings: 6 Ingredients:

- Four large tomatoes, sliced

- One can make coconut milk (14-oz)

- Six cloves garlic, crushed then minced

- One whole onion, sliced thinly

- 1tbsp curry

- 1 tbsp. turmeric

- 1 tsp. cinnamon

- 1 tsp. clove powder

- 1 tsp. fenugreek

- 1-inch long ginger around thumb-sized, peeled

- Two bay leaves

- 1/2 tsp. salt

- 1 tsp. pepper

- 2tbsp olive oil

- 2lbs. boneless and skinless chicken breasts cut into 1-inch cubes

- 2cups of water

- ¼ of the red bell pepper cut into 1-inch thick strips

Directions:

1. In a heavy-bottomed pot, heat oil on the medium-high fire.

2. Sauté garlic and ginger until garlic is starting to brown, around 1 to 2 minutes.

3. Add curry, turmeric, cinnamon, clove, bay leaf, and fenugreek. Sauté until fragrant, around 3 to 5 minutes.

4. Add tomatoes and onions. Sauté for 5 to ten minutes or until tomatoes are wilted, and onions are soft and translucent. If needed, add ¼ cup of water.

5. Add chicken breasts and sauté for 5 minutes—season with pepper and salt.

6. Add remaining water; bring to a boil, then slow fire to medium. While covered, continue cooking chicken for at least 15 minutes.

7. Add bell pepper and coconut milk. Cook until heated through.

8. Turn off fire and serve best with brown rice.

Nutrition: Calories 225, Total Fat 8g, Saturated Fat 1.6g, Total Carbs 12g, Net Carbs 10g, Protein 28g, Sugar: 4g, Fiber 2g, Sodium 1290mg, Potassium 782mg

9.   Turkey And Quinoa Stuffed Peppers

Preparation Time: 15 minutes

Cooking time: 35 minutes

Servings: 6

Ingredients:

- Three large red bell peppers
- 2tsp chopped fresh rosemary
- 2tbsp chopped fresh parsley
- 3tbsp chopped pecans, toasted
- 2 tbsp. extra virgin olive oil
- ½ cup chicken stock
- ½ lb. fully cooked smoked turkey sausage, diced
- ½ tsp. salt
- 2cups of water
- 1cup uncooked quinoa

Directions:

1. On high fire, place a large saucepan and add salt, water, and quinoa. Bring to a boil.

2. Once boiling, reduce fire to a simmer, cover, and cook until all water is absorbed, around 15 minutes.

3. Uncover quinoa, turn off the fire, and let it stand for another 5 minutes.

4. Add rosemary, parsley, pecans, olive oil, chicken stock, and turkey sausage into quinoa pan. Mix well.

5. Slice peppers lengthwise in half and discards membranes and seeds. In another boiling pot of water, add peppers, boil for 5 minutes, drain and discard water.

6. Grease a 13 x 9 baking dish and preheat oven to 350oF.

7. Place boiled bell pepper onto a prepared baking dish, evenly fill with the quinoa mixture, and pop into the oven.

8. Bake for 15 minutes.

Nutrition:

Calories 253, Total Fat 13g, Saturated Fat 2g, Total Carbs 21g, Net Carbs 19.7g, Protein 14g, Sugar: 1.3g, Fiber 3g, Sodium 545mg, Potassium 372mg

CHAPTER 5:

Sides

10.   Baked Vegetables

Preparation Time: 10 minutes

Cooking Time: 30 minutes

Serve: 6

Ingredients:

- Two zucchini, sliced

- Two tomatoes, quartered

- Six fresh basil leaves, sliced

- 2 tsp. Italian seasoning

- 2 tbsp. olive oil

- One eggplant, sliced

- One onion, sliced

- One bell pepper, cut into strips

- Pepper

- Salt

Directions:

1. Fit the Cuisinart oven with the rack in position 1.

2. Add all ingredients except basil leaves into the bowl and toss well.

3. Transfer vegetable mixture to parchment-lined baking pan.

4. Set to bake at 400 F for 35 minutes. After 5 minutes, place the baking pan in the preheated oven.

5. Garnish with basil and serve.

Nutrition:

Calories 96

Fat 5.5 g

Carbohydrates 11.7 g

Sugar 6.4 g

Protein 2.3 g

Cholesterol 1 mg

11. Cheese Herb Zucchini

Preparation Time: 10 minutes

Cooking Time: 15 minutes

Serve: 4

Ingredients:

- Four zucchini, quartered

- 1/2 tsp. dried oregano

- 2 tbsp. fresh parsley, chopped

- 2 tbsp. olive oil

- 1/2 tsp. dried thyme

- 1/2 cup parmesan cheese, grated

- 1/4 tsp. garlic powder

- 1/2 tsp. dried basil

- Pepper

- Salt

Directions:

1. Fit the Cuisinart oven with the rack in position 1.

2. In a small bowl, mix parmesan cheese, garlic powder, basil, oregano, thyme, pepper, and salt.

3. Arrange zucchini in baking pan and drizzle with oil, and sprinkle with parmesan cheese mixture.

4. Set to bake at 350 F for 20 minutes. After 5 minutes, place the baking pan in the preheated oven.

5. Garnish with parsley and serve.

Nutrition:

Calories 130

Fat 9.8 g

Carbohydrates 7.4 g

Sugar 3.5 g

Protein 6.1 g

Cholesterol 8 mg

12. Healthy Spinach Muffins

Preparation Time: 10 minutes

Cooking Time: 15 minutes

Serve: 12

Ingredients:

- Ten eggs
- 2 cups spinach, chopped
- 1/2 tsp. dried basil
- 1 1/2 cups parmesan cheese, grated
- 1/4 tsp. garlic powder
- 1/4 tsp. onion powder
- Salt

Directions:

1. Fit the Cuisinart oven with the rack in position 1.

2. Spray 12-cups muffin tin with cooking spray and set aside.

3. In a large bowl, whisk eggs with basil, garlic powder, onion powder, and salt.

4. Add cheese and spinach and stir well.

5. Pour egg mixture into the prepared muffin tin.

6.   Set to bake at 400 F for 20 minutes. After 5 minutes, place the muffin tin in the preheated oven.

7.   Serve and enjoy.

Nutrition:

Calories 90

Fat 6.1 g

Carbohydrates 0.9 g

Sugar 0.3 g

Protein 8.4 g

Cholesterol 144 mg

CHAPTER 6:

Seafood

13.   Salmon Dill Patties

Preparation Time: 10 minutes

Cooking Time: 15 minutes

Servings: 2

Ingredients:

- 1 egg

- 1 tsp. dill weeds

- 1/2 cup almond flour

- 14 oz. salmon

- 1/4 cup onion, diced

Directions:

1.   Place the air fryer Basket onto the Baking Pan and spray air fryer basket with cooking spray.

2.   Add all ingredients into the bowl and mix well.

3.   Make patties from bowl mixture and place onto the air fryer basket.

4.   Place assembled baking pan into Rack Position 2.

5.   Set to air fry at 375°F for 10 minutes.

6.   Serve and enjoy.

Nutrition:

Calories 350

Fat 18 g

Carbohydrates 3 g

Sugar 1 g

Protein 44 g

Cholesterol 172 mg

14.   Spicy Shrimp

Preparation Time: 10 minutes Cooking Time: 16 minutes

Servings: 2 Ingredients:

- 1/2 lb. shrimp, peeled and deveined
- 1/2 tsp. old bay seasoning
- 1/2 tsp. cayenne pepper
- 1 tbsp. olive oil
- 1/4 tsp. paprika
- Pinch of salt

Directions:

1.   Place the air fryer Basket onto the Baking Pan and spray air fryer basket with cooking spray.

2.   Add shrimp and remaining ingredients into the bowl and toss well to coat.

3.   Add shrimp into the air fryer basket.

4.   Place assembled baking pan into Rack Position 2.

5.   Set to air fry at 400°F for 6 minutes.

6.   Serve and enjoy.

Nutrition:Calories 197 Fat 9 g Carbohydrates 2 g Sugar 0.1 g

Protein 26 g Cholesterol 239 mg

15.   Air Fried White Fish Fillet

Preparation Time: 10 minutes

Cooking Time: 20 minutes

Servings: 2

Ingredients:

- 12 oz. white fish fillets

- 1/2 tsp. lemon pepper seasoning

- 1/2 tsp. garlic powder

- 1/2 tsp. onion powder

- Pepper

- Salt

Directions:

1. Place the air fryer Basket onto the Baking Pan and spray air fryer basket with cooking spray.

2. Spray fish fillets with cooking spray and season with onion powder, lemon pepper seasoning, garlic powder, pepper, and salt.

3. Place parchment paper in the bottom of the air fryer basket.

4. Place fish fillets into the air fryer basket.

5. Place assembled baking pan into Rack Position 2.

6. Set to air fry at 350°F for 10 minutes.

7. Serve and enjoy.

Nutrition:

Calories 298

Fat 13 g

Carbohydrates 1.4 g

Sugar 0.4 g

Protein 42 g

Cholesterol 131 mg

16.   Mustard-Crusted Sole Fillets

Preparation Time: 5 minutes

Cooking time: 10 minutes

Servings: 4

Ingredients:

- Five teaspoons low-sodium yellow mustard

- One tablespoon freshly squeezed lemon juice

- 4 (3.5-ounce / 99-g) sole fillets

- Two teaspoons olive oil

- ½ teaspoon dried marjoram

- ½ teaspoon dried thyme

- ⅛ teaspoon freshly ground black pepper

- One slice low-sodium whole-wheat bread, crumbled

Directions:

1. Whisk together the mustard and lemon juice in a small bowl until thoroughly mixed and smooth. Spread the mixture evenly over the sole fillets, and then transfer the fillets to the air fry basket.

2. In a separate bowl, combine the olive oil, marjoram, thyme, black pepper, and bread crumbs and stir to mix well. Gently

but firmly press the mixture onto the top of fillets, coating them completely.

3. Select Bake, Convection, set temperature to 320°F (160°C), and set time to 10 minutes. Select Start to begin preheating.

4. Once preheated, place the basket on the bake position.

5. When cooking is complete, the fish should reach an internal temperature of 145°F (63°C) on a meat thermometer. Remove the basket from the oven and serve on a plate.

17. Sole And Cauliflower Fritters

Preparation Time: 5 minutes

Cooking time: 24 minutes

Servings: 2

Ingredients:

- ½ pound (227 g) sole fillets

- ½ pound (227 g) mashed cauliflower

- ½ cup red onion, chopped

- One bell pepper, finely chopped

- One egg, beaten

- Two garlic cloves, minced

- Two tablespoons fresh parsley, chopped

- One tablespoon olive oil

- One tablespoon coconut amino

- ½ teaspoon scotch bonnet pepper, minced

- ½ teaspoon paprika

- Salt and white pepper, to taste

- Cooking spray

Directions:

1. Spray the air fry basket with cooking spray. Place the sole fillets in the basket.

2. Select Air Fry, Convection, set temperature to 395°F (202°C), and set time to 10 minutes. Select Start to begin preheating.

3. Once preheated, place the basket on the air fry position. Flip the fillets halfway through.

4. When cooking is complete, transfer the fish fillets to a large bowl. Mash the fillets into flakes. Add the remaining ingredients and stir to combine.

5. Make the patties: Scoop out two tablespoons of the fish mixture and shape into a patty about ½ inches thick with your hands. Repeat with the remaining fish mixture. Place the cakes in the air fry basket.

6. Select Bake, Convection, set temperature to 380°F (193°C), and set time to 14 minutes. Select Start to begin preheating.

7. Once preheated, place the basket on the bake position. Flip the patties halfway through.

8. When cooking is complete, they should be golden brown and cooked through. Remove the basket from the oven and cool for 5 minutes before serving.

18.　Parmesan-Crusted Salmon Patties

Preparation Time: 10 minutes

Cooking time: 13 minutes

Servings: 4

Ingredients:

- 1 pound (454 g) salmon, chopped into ½-inch pieces

- Two tablespoons coconut flour

- Two tablespoons grated Parmesan cheese

- 1½ tablespoons milk

- ½ white onion, peeled and finely chopped

- ½ teaspoon butter, at room temperature

- ½ teaspoon chipotle powder

- ½ teaspoon dried parsley flakes

- ⅓ teaspoon ground black pepper

- ⅓ teaspoon smoked cayenne pepper

- One teaspoon acceptable sea salt

Directions:

1.　Put all the ingredients for the salmon patties in a bowl and stir to combine well.

2.   Scoop out two tablespoons of the salmon mixture and shape into a patty with your palm, about ½ inches thick. Repeat until all the combination is used. Transfer to the refrigerator for about 2 hours until firm.

3.   When ready, arrange the salmon patties in the air fry basket.

4.   Select Bake, Convection, set temperature to 395°F (202°C), and set time to 13 minutes. Select Start to begin preheating.

5.   Once preheated, place the basket on the bake position. Flip the patties halfway through the cooking time.

6.   When cooking is complete, the patties should be golden brown. Remove from the oven and cool for 5 minutes before serving.

CHAPTER 7:

Poultry

19. Crisp Chicken W/ Mustard Vinaigrette

Preparation Time: 15 minutes

Cooking Time: 10 minutes

Servings: 1

Ingredients

Salad:

- 250g chicken breast

- 1 cup shaved Brussels sprouts

- 2 cups baby spinach

- 2 cups mixed greens

- 1/2 avocado sliced

- Segments of one orange

- 1 teaspoon raw pumpkin seeds

- 1 teaspoon toasted almonds

- 1 teaspoon hemp seeds

- Dressing:

- 1/2 shallot, chopped

- 1 garlic clove, chopped

- 2 teaspoons balsamic vinegar

- 1 teaspoon extra virgin olive oil

- ½ cup fresh orange juice

- 1 teaspoon Dijon mustard

- 1 teaspoon raw honey

- Fresh ground pepper

Directions

1. In a blender, blend all dressing ingredients until very smooth; set aside.

2. Set your air fryer toast oven to 350 degrees and brush the basket of the air fryer toast oven with oil.

3. Place the chicken breast on the basket and cook for10 minutes, 5 minutes per side.

4. Take out of the air fryer toast oven and transfer to a plate. Let sit for 5 minutes then cut into bite-sized chunks.

5. Combine all salad ingredients in a large bowl; drizzle with dressing and toss to coat well before serving.

Nutrition:

Calories: 457 kcal,

Carbs: 13.6 g,

Fat: 37 g,

Protein: 31.8 g.

20. Chicken With Oregano-Orange Chimichurri & Arugula Salad

Preparation Time: 5 minutes

Cooking Time:: 12 minutes

Servings: 4

Ingredients

- 1 teaspoon finely grated orange zest

- 1 teaspoon dried oregano

- 1 small garlic clove, grated

- 2 teaspoon vinegar (red wine, cider, or white wine)

- 1 tablespoon fresh orange juice

- 1/2 cup chopped fresh flat-leaf parsley leaves

- 700g chicken breast, cut into 4 pieces

- Sea salt and pepper

- 1/4 cup and 2 teaspoons extra virgin olive oil

- 4 cups arugula

- 2 bulbs fennel, shaved

- 2 tablespoons whole-grain mustard

Directions

1. Make chimichurri: In a medium bowl, combine orange zest, oregano, and garlic. Mix in vinegar, orange juice, and parsley and then slowly whisk in ¼ cup of olive oil until emulsified. Season with sea salt and pepper.

2. Sprinkle the chicken with salt and pepper and set your air fryer toast oven to 350 degrees F.

3. Brush the chicken steaks with the remaining olive oil and cook for about 6 minutes per side or until evenly browned. Take out from the fryer and let rest for at least 10 minutes.

4. Toss the cooked chicken, greens, and fennel with mustard in a medium bowl; season with salt and pepper.

5. Serve steak with chimichurri and salad. Enjoy!

Nutrition:

Calories: 312 kcal

Carbs: 12.8 g

Fat: 33.6 g

Protein: 29 g

21.   Stir-Fried Chicken With Water Chestnuts

Preparation Time: 10 minutes

Cooking Time: 15 minutes

Servings: 4

Ingredients

- 2 tablespoons sesame oil

- ¼ cup wheat-free tamari

- 4 small chicken breasts, sliced

- 1 small cabbage, chopped

- 3 garlic cloves, chopped

- 1 teaspoon Chinese five-spice powder

- 1 cup dried plums

- 1 cup water chestnuts

- Toasted sesame seeds

Directions

1. Start by preheating your air fryer toast oven at 370 degrees F.

2. Heat sesame oil in your air fryer toast oven's pan set over medium heat; stir in all the ingredients, except sesame seeds, and transfer to the air fryer toast oven.

3. Cook until cabbage and chicken are tender for 15-20 minutes.

4. Serve warm sprinkled with toasted sesame seeds.

5. Enjoy!

Nutrition:

Calories: 404 kcal,

Carbs: 11.3 g,

Fat: 29 g,

Protein: 22 g.

22.   Perfectly Fried Chicken Roast Served With Fruit Compote

Preparation Time: 15 minutes

Cooking Time: 50 minutes

Servings: 12

Ingredients:

- 1 full chicken, dissected

- 2 tablespoons extra virgin olive oil

- 2 tablespoons chopped garlic

- 2 teaspoons sea salt

- 1 teaspoon pepper

- 1 tablespoon chopped fresh thyme

- 1 tablespoon chopped fresh rosemary

- Fruit Compote

- 1 apple, diced

- 1/2 cup red grapes, halved, seeds removed

- 12 dried apricots, sliced

- 16 dried figs, coarsely chopped

- 1/2 cup chopped red onion

- 1/2 cup cider vinegar

- 1/2 cup dry white wine

- 2 teaspoons liquid stevia

- 1/2 teaspoon salt

- 1/2 teaspoon pepper

Directions

1. In a small bowl, stir together thyme, rosemary, garlic, salt, and pepper and rub the mixture over the pork.

2. Light your air fryer toast oven and set it to 320°F, place the chicken on the basket and cook for 10 minutes.

3. Increase the temperature and cook for another 10 minutes, turning the chicken pieces once. Increase the temperature one more time to 400 degrees F and cook for 5 minutes to get a crispy finish.

4. Make Fruit Compote: In a saucepan, combine all ingredients and cook over medium heat, stirring, for about 25 minutes or until liquid is reduced to a quarter.

5. Once the chicken is cooked, serve hot with a spoon of fruit compote Enjoy!

Nutrition: Calories: 511 kcal, Carbs: 15 g, Fat: 36.8 g,

Protein: 31.5 g.

23.   Lemon Pepper Chicken Legs

Preparation Time: 20 minutes Cooking Time: 30 minutes

 Servings: 2

Ingredients:

- ½ tsp. garlic powder

- 2tsp. baking powder

- Eight chicken legs

- 1tbsp. salted butter, melted

- 1tbsp. lemon-pepper seasoning

Directions:

1. In a small bowl, combine the garlic powder and baking powder, and then use this mixture to coat the chicken legs. Lay the chicken in the basket of your fryer.

2. Cook the chicken legs at 375°F for twenty-five minutes. Halfway through, turn them over and allow them to cook on the other side.

3. When the chicken has turned golden brown, test with a thermometer to ensure it has reached an ideal temperature of 165°F. Remove from the fryer.

4. Mix the melted butter and lemon pepper seasoning, and toss with the chicken legs until the chicken is coated. Serve hot.

CHAPTER 8:

Meat

24. Hot Flank Steaks With Roasted Peanuts

Preparation Time: 10minutes

Cooking time: 35 minutes

Servings: 3 to 4

Ingredients:

- 2 lb. flank steaks, cut into long strips

- 2 tbsp. fish sauce

- 2 tbsp. soy sauce

- 2 tbsp. sugar

- 2 tbsp. ground garlic

- 2 tbsp. ground ginger

- 2 tsp. hot sauce

- 1 cup chopped cilantro, divided into two

- ½ cup roasted peanuts, chopped

Directions:

1. Preheat the Air Fryer to 400 F. In a zipper bag, add the beef, fish sauce, swerve sweetener, garlic, soy sauce, ginger, half of the cilantro, and hot sauce. Zip the bag and massage the Ingredients: with your hands to mix well.

2. Open the bag, remove the beef, shake off the excess marinade, place the beef strips in the fryer basket in a single layer, and avoid overlapping. Close the Air Fryer and cook for 5 minutes.

3. Turn the beef and cook further for 5 minutes.

4. Dish the cooked meat in a serving platter, garnish with the peanuts and the remaining cilantro.

25. Authentic Wiener Beef Schnitzel

Preparation Time: 10 minutes

Cooking Time: 25 minutes

Serving: 4

Ingredients:

- 4beef schnitzel cutlets

- ½ cup flour

- 2eggs, beaten

- Salt and black pepper

- 1cup breadcrumbs

Directions:

1. Coat the cutlets in flour and shake off any excess. Dip the coated cutlets into the beaten egg. Sprinkle with salt and black pepper. Then dip into the crumbs and to cover well. Spray them generously with oil and cook for 10 minutes at 360 F, turning once halfway through.

26. Dreamy Beef Steak With Rice, Broccoli And Green Beans

Preparation Time: 40 minutes

Servings: 2

Ingredients:

- 1lb beef steak,

- Salt and black pepper to taste to season

Fried Rice:

- 2½ cups of rice

- 1½ tbsp. soy sauce

- 2tsp sesame oil

- 2tsp minced ginger

- 2tsp vinegar

- One clove garlic, minced

- ¼ cup chopped broccoli

- ¼ cup green beans

Directions:

1. Put the beef on a chopping board and use a knife to cut it into 2-inch strips. Add the meat to a bowl, sprinkle with pepper and salt, and mix it with a spoon. Let it sit for 10 minutes.

Preheat the Air Fryer to 400 F. Add the beef to the fryer basket, and cook for 5 minutes. Turn the beef strips with kitchen tongs and cook further for 3 minutes.

2. Once ready, remove the beef to a safe-oven dish that fits in the fryer's basket. Add the rice, broccoli, green beans, garlic, ginger, sesame oil, vinegar, and soy sauce. Mix evenly using a spoon.

3. Place the dish in the fryer basket, close, and cook at 370 F for 10 minutes. Open the Air Fryer, mix the rice well, and cook for 4 minutes; season with salt and pepper. Dish the rice into serving bowls and serve with hot sauce.

27.   Mustard Pork Chops With Lemon Zest

Preparation Time: 10 minutes

Cooking time: 25 minutes

Servings: 3

Ingredients:

- Three lean pork chops

- Salt and black pepper to taste to season

- Two eggs, cracked into a bowl

- 1tbsp water

- 1cup breadcrumbs

- ½ tsp. garlic powder

- 3 tsp. paprika

- 1½ tsp. Oregano

- ½ tsp. Cayenne pepper

- ¼ tsp. dry mustard

- One lemon, zested

Directions:

1.   Put the pork chops on a chopping board and use a knife to trim off any excess fat. Add the water to the

eggs and whisk; set aside. In another bowl, add the breadcrumbs, salt, pepper, garlic powder, paprika, oregano, cayenne pepper, lemon zest, and dry mustard. Use a fork to mix evenly.

2. Preheat the Air Fryer to 380 F and grease the basket with cooking spray. In the egg mixture, dip each pork chop and then in the breadcrumb mixture. Place the breaded chops in the fryer. Don't spray with cooking spray. The fat in the chops will be enough oil to cook them. Close the Air Fryer and cook for 12 minutes.

3. Flip to other side and cook for another 5 minutes.

4. Once ready, place the chops on a chopping board to rest for 3 minutes before slicing and serving. Serve with a side of vegetable fries.

28. Herbed Beef Roast

Preparation Time: 10 minutes Cooking time: 50 minutes

Servings: 2 Ingredients:

- 2 tsp. olive oil

- 1 lb. beef roast

- ½ tsp. Dried rosemary

- ½ tsp. Dried thyme

- ½ tsp. dried oregano

- Salt and black pepper to taste

Directions:

1. Preheat the Air Fryer to 400 F. Drizzle oil over the beef, and sprinkle with salt, pepper, and herbs. Rub onto the meat with hands.

2. Cook for 45 minutes for medium-rare and 50 minutes for well-done.

3. Check halfway through, and flip to ensure they cook evenly.

4. Wrap the beef in foil for 10 minutes after cooking to allow the juices to reabsorb into the meat. Slice the beef and serve with a side of steamed asparagus.

29.   Roast Pork Belly With Cumin

Preparation: 15 minutes

Cooking time: 4 hours and 30 minutes

Servings: 8

Ingredients:

- 1½ lb. pork belly

- 1½ tsp. Garlic powder

- ½ tsp. Coriander powder

- ⅓ tsp. Salt

- ½ tsp. Black pepper

- ½ dried thyme

- ½ tsp. dried oregano

- 1½ tsp. cumin powder

- 3 cups of water

- lemon halved

Directions:

1.   Leave the pork to air fry for 3 hours. In a small bowl, add the garlic powder, coriander powder, ½ tsp. of salt, black pepper, thyme, oregano, and cumin powder.

After the pork is well dried, poke holes all around it using a fork. Smear the oregano, rub thoroughly on all sides with your hands, and squeeze the lemon juice all over it.

2.   Leave to sit for 5 minutes. Put the pork in the center of the fryer basket and cook for 30 minutes. Turn the pork with two spatulas, increase the temperature to 350 F and continue cooking for 25 minutes.

3.   Once ready, remove it and place it on a chopping board to sit for 4 minutes before slicing. Serve the pork slices with a side of sautéed asparagus and hot sauce.

30.   Sunday Night Garlic Beef Schnitzel

Preparation Time: 8minutes

Cooking time: 22 minutes

Servings: 1

Ingredients:

- 2 tbsp. olive oil

- One thin beef cutlet

- One egg, beaten

- 2 oz. breadcrumbs

- 1tsp paprika

- ¼ tsp. garlic powder

- Salt and black pepper to taste

Directions:

1.   Preheat the air fryer to 350 F. Combine olive oil, breadcrumbs, paprika, garlic powder, and salt in a bowl. Dip the beef in with the egg first, and then coat it with the breadcrumb mixture thoroughly.

2.   Line a baking dish with parchment paper and place the breaded meat on it.

3.   Cook for 12 minutes. Serve and enjoy.

CHAPTER 9:

Vegetables

31. Garlicky Cauliflower Florets

Preparation Time: 5 minutes

Cooking Time: 20 minutes

Serve: 4

Ingredients:

- 5 cups cauliflower florets

- 1/2 tsp. cumin powder

- 1/2 tsp. coriander powder

- Six garlic cloves, chopped

- Four tablespoons olive oil

- 1/2 tsp. salt

Directions:

1. Add all ingredients into the large bowl and toss well.

2. Add cauliflower florets into the air fryer basket.

3.   Place air fryer basket into the oven, and select air fry mode. Set Omni to 400 F for 20 minutes. Stir twice.

4.   Serve and enjoy.

Nutrition:

Calories 159

Fat 14.2 g

Carbohydrates 8.2 g

Sugar 3.1 g

Protein 2.8 g

Cholesterol 0 mg

32.   Flavors Green Beans

Preparation Time: 5 minutes

Cooking Time: 10 minutes

Serve: 2

Ingredients:

- 2 cups green beans
- 1/8 tsp. cayenne pepper
- 1/8 tsp. ground allspice
- 1/4 tsp. ground cinnamon
- 1/2 tsp. dried oregano
- 2 tbsp. olive oil
- 1/4 tsp. ground coriander
- 1/4 tsp. ground cumin
- 1/2 tsp. salt

Directions:

1.   Add all ingredients into the mixing bowl and toss well.

2.   Spray air fryer basket with cooking spray.

3.   Add bowl mixture into the air fryer basket.

4.   Place air fryer basket into the oven, and select air fry mode; set Omni to 370 F for 10 minutes.

5.   Serve and enjoy.

Nutrition:

Calories 158

Fat 14.3 g

Carbohydrates 8.6 g

Sugar 1.6 g

Protein 2.1 g

Cholesterol 0 mg

33.   Potato Casserole

Preparation Time: 5 minutes

Cooking Time: 35 minutes

Serve: 6

Ingredients:

- Five eggs

- 1/2 cup cheddar cheese, shredded

- Two medium potatoes, diced into 1/2-inch cubes

- One green bell pepper, diced

- One onion, chopped

- 1 tbsp. olive oil

- 3/4 tsp. pepper

- 3/4 tsp. salt

Directions:

1.   Spray 9*9-inch casserole dish with cooking spray and set aside.

2.   Heat olive oil in a large pan over medium heat.

3.   Add onion and sauté for 1 minute. Add potatoes, bell peppers, ½ tsp. Black pepper, and 1.2 tsp. Salt and sauté for 4 minutes more or until onions are softened.

4.   Transfer sautéed vegetables to the prepared casserole dish and spread evenly.

5.   In a bowl, whisk eggs, and remaining pepper and salt.

6.   Pour egg mixture into the casserole dish and sprinkle cheddar cheese on top.

7.   Select bake mode and set the Omni to 350 F for 35 minutes. Once the oven beeps, place the casserole dish into the oven.

8.   Serve and enjoy.

Nutrition:

Calories 174

Fat 9.2 g

Carbohydrates 14.9 g

Sugar 2.9 g

Protein 8.6 g

Cholesterol 146 mg

34. Zucchini Egg Bake

Preparation Time: 5 minutes

Cooking Time: 30 minutes

Serve: 4

Ingredients:

- Six eggs

- 1/2 tsp. dill

- 1/2 tsp. oregano

- 1/2 tsp. basil

- 1/2 tsp. baking powder

- 1/2 cup almond flour

- 1 cup cheddar cheese, shredded

- 1 cup kale, chopped

- One onion, chopped

- 1 cup zucchini, shredded and squeezed out all liquid

- 1/2 cup milk

- 1/4 tsp. salt

Directions:

1. Grease 9*9-inch baking dish and set aside.

2.   In a large bowl, whisk eggs with milk.

3.   Add remaining ingredients and stir until well combined.

4.   Pour egg mixture into the prepared baking dish.

5.   Select bake mode and set the Omni to 375 F for 30 minutes once the oven beeps, place the baking dish into the oven.

6.   Serve and enjoy.

Nutrition:

Calories 269

Fat 18.4 g

Carbohydrates 8.9 g

Sugar 3.8 g

Protein 18.3 g

Cholesterol 278 mg

35.   Balsamic Baked Mushrooms

Preparation Time: 5 minutes

Cooking Time: 20 minutes

Serve: 6

Ingredients:

- 1 lb. button mushrooms, scrubbed and stems trimmed

- 2 tbsp. olive oil

- 4 tbsp. balsamic vinegar

- 1/2 tsp. dried basil

- 1/2 tsp. dried oregano

- Three garlic cloves, crushed

- 1/4 tsp. black pepper

- 1 tsp. sea salt

Directions:

1.   Spray a cooking pan with cooking spray and set aside.

2.   In a large bowl, whisk together vinegar, basil, oregano, garlic, olive oil, pepper, and salt.

3.   Stir in mushrooms and let sit for 15 minutes.

4.   Spread mushrooms onto the prepared cooking pan.

5.   Select bake mode and set the Omni to 425 F for 20 minutes once the oven beeps, place the cooking pan into the oven.

6.   Serve and enjoy.

Nutrition:

Calories 61

Fat 4.9 g

Carbohydrates 3.2 g

Sugar 1.4 g

Protein 2.5 g

Cholesterol 0 mg

CHAPTER 10:

Soup

36.   Barley Beef Soup

Preparation Time: 35 minutes

Cooking Time: 30 minutes

Servings: 4

Ingredients:

- 12 oz. beef stew meat, cut into
- inch cubes one medium leek, chopped
- garlic cloves, chopped
- bay leaves
- can tomatoes (15 oz.), diced and drained
- 1/2 cup barley
- 1 cup of frozen mixed vegetables
- cups beef broth
- tbsp. extra virgin olive oil

- 1 tsp. paprika

Directions:

1. Heat oil in a large saucepan over medium-high heat. Sauté beef until well browned. Add in leeks and garlic and sauté until fragrant.

2. Add paprika, beef broth, and bay leaves; season with salt and pepper.

3. Cover and bring to a boil, then reduce heat and simmer for 60 minutes. Stir in frozen vegetables, tomatoes, and barley.

4. Return to boiling, reduce heat, and simmer, covered, about 15 minutes more or until meat and vegetables are tender. Discard bay leaves and serve.

37. Italian Vegetable Soup

Preparation Time: 35 minutes

Cooking Time: 20 minutes

Servings: 4

Ingredients:

- 1/2 onion, chopped

- Two garlic cloves, chopped

- ¼ cabbage, chopped

- 3 cups water; 1 carrot, chopped

- Two celery stalks, chopped

- One cup canned tomatoes, diced, undrained

- One and a half cup green beans, trimmed and cut into

- 1/2-inch pieces

- 1/2 cup pasta, cooked

- 2-3 fresh basil leaves

- 2 tbsp. extra virgin olive oil

- black pepper and salt to taste

Directions:

1. Heat the olive oil in a large pot over medium-high heat.

2.   Add the onion and cook until translucent, about 4 minutes.

3.   Add in the garlic, carrot, and celery and cook for 5 minutes more.

4.   Stir in the green beans, cabbage, tomatoes, basil, and water and bring to a boil.

5.   Reduce heat and simmer uncovered for 15 minutes or until vegetables are tender. Stir in pasta, season with pepper and salt to taste, and serve.

CHAPTER 11:

Snacks

38.   Buffalo Quesadillas

Preparation Time: 5 minutes

Cooking time: 5 minutes

Servings: 8

Ingredients:

- Nonstick cooking spray

- 2 cups chicken, cooked & chopped fine

- ½ cup Buffalo wing sauce

- 2 cups Monterey Jack cheese, grated

- ½ cup green onions, sliced thin

- Eight flour tortillas, 8-inch diameter

- ¼ cup blue cheese dressing

Directions:

1.   Lightly spray the baking pan with cooking spray.

2.   In a medium bowl, add chicken and wing sauce and toss to coat.

3.   Place tortillas, one at a time, on the work surface. Spread ¼ of the chicken mixture over tortilla and sprinkle with cheese and onion. Top with a second tortilla and place on the baking pan.

4.   Set oven to broil at 400°F for 8 minutes. After 5 minutes, place the baking pan in position 2. Cook quesadillas 2-3 minutes per side until toasted and cheese has melted. Repeat with the remaining ingredients.

5.   Cut quesadillas in wedges and serve with blue cheese dressing or other dipping sauce.

Nutrition:

Calories 376, Total Fat 20g, Saturated Fat 8g, Total Carbs 27g, Net Carbs 26g, Protein 22g, Sugar 2g, Fiber 2g, Sodium 685mg, Potassium 201mg, Phosphorus 301mg

39.   Crispy Sausage Bites

Preparation Time: 5 minutes

Cooking time: 15 minutes

Servings: 12

Ingredients:

- Nonstick cooking spray

- 2 lbs. spicy pork sausage

- 1 ½ cups Bisques

- 4 cups sharp cheddar cheese, grated

- ½ cup onion diced fine

- 2 tsp. pepper

- 2 tsp. garlic, chopped fine

Directions:

1.   Lightly spray the baking pan with cooking spray.

2.   In a large bowl, combine all ingredients. Form into 1-inch balls and place them on the baking pan. These will need to be cooked in batches.

3.   Set oven to bake at 375°F for 20 minutes. After 5 minutes, place baking pan in position two and cook 12-15 minutes

or until golden brown. Repeat with remaining sausage bites. Serve immediately.

Nutrition

Calories 432, Total Fat 32g, Saturated Fat 13g, Total Carbs 14g, Net Carbs 14g, Protein 22g, Sugar 1g, Fiber 0g, Sodium 803mg, Potassium 286mg, Phosphorus 298mg

40.   Puffed Asparagus Spears

Preparation Time: 20 minutes

Cooking time: 20 minutes

Servings: 10

Ingredients:

- Nonstick cooking spray

- 3 oz. prosciutto, sliced thin & cut into 30 long strips

- 30 asparagus spears, trimmed

- 10 (14 x 9-inch) sheets phyllo dough, thawed

Directions:

1.   Place the baking pan in position 2 of the oven.

2.   Wrap each asparagus spear with a piece of prosciutto, like a barber pole.

3.   One at a time, place a sheet of phyllo on a work surface and cut into 3 4 1/2x9-inch rectangles.

4.   Place an asparagus spear across a short end and roll-up— place in a single layer in the fryer basket. Spray with cooking spray.

5.   Place the basket in the oven and set it to air fry at 450°F for 10 minutes. Cook until phyllo is crisp and golden,

about 8-10 minutes, turning over halfway through cooking time. Repeat with the remaining ingredients. Serve warm.

Nutrition

Calories 74, Total Fat 2g, Saturated Fat 0g, Total Carbs 11g, Net Carbs 10g, Protein 3g, Sugar 0g, Fiber 1g, Sodium 189mg, Potassium 60mg, Phosphorus 33mg

41. Rabas Is A Hot Air Fryer

Preparation Time: 10 minutes

Cooking time: 35 minutes

Servings: 4

Ingredients

- 16 rabas

- One egg

- Bread crumbs

- Condiments: salt, pepper, sweet paprika

Directions:

1. In my case, they were frozen, so I put them in hot water, and they boil for 2 minutes.

2. Remove and dry well.

3. Beat the egg and season to taste. I put salt, pepper, and sweet paprika—place in the egg.

4. Bread with breadcrumbs. Place in sticks.

5. Place in the fryer for 5 minutes at 160 degrees. Remove

Spray with fritolin and place five more minutes at 200 degrees

CHAPTER 12:

Desserts

42.   Air Fried Butter Cake

Preparation Time: 10 minutes

Cooking Time: 15 minutes

Serving: 4

This is a basic butter cake you can easily prepare in the air fryer.

Ingredients:

- Cooking spray

- 7 Tablespoons of butter, at ambient temperature

- White sugar: ¼ cup plus 2 tablespoons

- 1 Ok.

- All-purpose flour: 1 ⅔ cups

- Salt: 1 pinch or to taste

- Milk: 6 tablespoons

Directions:

1. Preheat an air fryer to 350 F (180 C). Spray the cooking spray on a tiny fluted tube pan.

2. Take a large bowl and add ¼ cup butter and 2 tablespoons of sugar in it.

3. Take an electric mixer to beat the sugar and butter until smooth and fluffy. Stir in salt and flour. Stir in the milk and thoroughly combine batter. Move batter to the prepared saucepan; use a spoon back to level the surface.

4. Place the pan inside the basket of the air fryer. Set the timer within 15 minutes. Bake the batter until a toothpick comes out clean when inserted into the cake.

5. Turn the cake out of the saucepan and allow it to cool for about five minutes.

Nutrition:

Per Serving: 470 calories| 22.4 g total fat| 102 mg cholesterol| 210 mg sodium| 59.7 g carbohydrates| 7.9 g protein;

43.　Chocolate Chip Cookies

Preparation Time: 15 minutes

Cooking Time: 5 minutes

Serving: 30 cookies

Ingredients:

- Unsalted butter: 2 sticks (1 cup)

- Dark brown sugar: ¾ cup

- ¾ tablespoon of dark brown sugar

- Vanilla extract: 2 tablespoon

- 2 Big Eggs

- Kosher salt: 1 teaspoon

- Baking soda: 1 teaspoon

- All-purpose flour: 2 1/3 cups

- 2 Cups of chocolate chips

- Chopped walnuts: 3/4 cups

- Cooking spray

- Flaky sea salt , for garnish (optional)

Directions:

1. Take a large bowl and add unsalted butter in it. Beat the butter with an electric hand mixer. Add 3/4 cup of granulated sugar with 3/4 cup of dark brown sugar and beat at normal speed for 2 to 3 minutes.

2. Add 1 spoonful of vanilla extract, 2 large eggs and 1 tablespoon of kosher salt, and beat until mixed. Add in increments 1 tablespoon baking soda and 2 1/3 cups of all-purpose flour, stirring until it is just mixed.

3. Add 2 cups of chocolate chip chunks and 3/4 cup of chopped walnuts and stir until well combined with a rubber spatula.

4. Preheat the air Fryer to bake at 350°F and set aside for 5 minutes. Line the air fryer racks with parchment paper, making sure to leave space for air to circulate on all sides.

5. Drop the dough's 2-tablespoon scoops onto the racks, spacing them 1 "apart. Gently flatten each scoop to form a cookie. If you like, sprinkle with flaky sea salt. Bake for about 5 minutes, until golden brown. Remove the air fryer's racks and set it to cool for 3 to 5 minutes. Repeat with leftover dough. Serve warm.

Recipe Notes:

Storage: The leftovers can be kept at room temperature up to 3 days in an airtight container.

Nutrition

Per serving, based on 18 servings. (% daily value)

Calories: 330| Fat: 17.5 g (26.9%)| Saturated: 8.5 g (42.7%)| Carbs: 42.9 g (14.3%)| Fiber: 1.9 g (7.6%)| Sugars: 28.0 g| Protein: 4.0 g (8.0%)| Sodium: 172.1 mg (7.2%)

44.   Air Fryer S'mores

Preparation Time: 5 minutes

Cooking Time: 5 minutes

Serving: 4

Use your air fryer to make perfect, decadent s'mores treats! No requisite campfire!

Ingredients:

- Four graham crackers (each half split to make 2 squares, for a total of 8 squares)

- 8 Squares of Hershey's chocolate bar, broken into squares

- 4 Marshmallows

Directions:

1. Take deliberate steps. Air-fryers use hot air for cooking food. Marshmallows are light and fluffy, and this should keep the marshmallows from flying around the basket if you follow these steps.

2. Put 4 squares of graham crackers on a basket of the air fryer.

3. Place 2 squares of chocolate bars on each cracker.

4. Place back the basket in the air fryer and fry on air at 390 °F for 1 minute. It is barely long enough for the chocolate to melt. Remove basket from air fryer.

5. Top with a marshmallow over each cracker. Throw the marshmallow down a little bit into the melted chocolate. This will help to make the marshmallow stay over the chocolate.

6. Put back the basket in the air fryer and fry at 390 °F for 2 minutes. (The marshmallows should be puffed up and browned at the tops.)

7. Using tongs to carefully remove each cracker from the air fryer's basket and place it on a platter. Top each marshmallow with another square of graham crackers.

8. Enjoy it right away!

45.   Double-Glazed Cinnamon Biscuit Bites

This delicious cross between cinnamon rolls and biscuits is more straightforward than either. It stars a plain, no-yeast dough that doesn't need to rise and bakes in a matter of minutes into tender, fluffy bits.

Preparation Time: 40 minutes

Cooking Time: 25 minutes

Serving: 8

Ingredients:

- All-purpose flour: 2/3 cup (approx. 2 7/8 oz.)

- 1/4 teaspoon cinnamon

- 2 tablespoons of granulated sugar

- 1 teaspoon baking powder

- 1/4 teaspoon kosher salt

- Whole-wheat flour: 2/3 cup (approx. 2 2/3 oz.)

- 4 tablespoons of cold salted butter, cut into small pieces

- Whole milk: 1/3 cup

- Cooking spray

- Powdered sugar: 2 cups (approx. 8 oz.)

- Water: 3 tablespoons

Directions:

1. Take a medium-sized bowl; whisk the flours together, granulated sugar, baking powder, cinnamon, and salt.

2. Add butter; use 2 knives or a pastry cutter to cut into mixture until butter is well mixed with flour and mixture resembles coarse cornmeal. Add milk, then stir until dough forms a ball.

3. Place the dough on a floured surface and knead for about 30 seconds until it is smooth, forming a cohesive disk. Cut the dough into 16 pieces equal to each other. Wrap each piece gently into a smooth ball.

4. Coat air fryer basket with spray to cook well. Place 8 balls in a basket, leave room between each; spray the donut balls with the spray for cooking. Cook for 10 to 12 minutes, at 350 ° F until browned and puffed.

5. Remove the donut balls gently from the basket, and place over foil on a wire rack. Keep it cool for 5 minutes. Repeat the same process with remaining donut balls.

6. Whisk the caster sugar and water together until smooth in a medium cup. Spoon half of the glaze gently over donut sticks. Let cool for 5 minutes; glaze again, allowing excess to drip away.

Nutrition: Calories 325| Fat 7 g| Sat fat 4 g| Unsaturated fat 3 g| Protein 8 g| Carbohydrate 60 g| Fiber 5 g| Added Sugars 18 g| Calcium 17 g| Sodium 67 mg| Calcium 10%| DV Potassium 4%

46. Apple Cider Donuts

Preparation Time: 25 minutes

Cooking Time: 45 minutes

Serving: 18 Donuts

Yield: 18 Donuts | Prep Time: 25 minutes | Cooking Time: 45 minutes

Ingredients:

For the donuts:

- 2 Cups of apple cider

- All-purpose flour: 3 cups

- Medium brown sugar: ½ cup

- Baking powder: 2 teaspoons

- Ground cinnamon: 1 teaspoon

- Ground ginger: 1 teaspoon

- Baking soda: ½ teaspoon

- Kosher salt: ½ teaspoon

- 8 Tablespoons of cold unsalted butter (1 stick)

- 1/2 cup frozen milk

For finishing and shaping:

- All-purpose flour: ¼ cup

- Unsalted butter: 8 tablespoons

- Granulated sugar: 1 cup

- 1 Teaspoon cinnamon

Directions:

1. Dough preparation: Pour 2 cups of apple cider into a small saucepan over medium-high heat and bring to a boil. Boil until half (to 1 cup) is reduced, for 10 to 12 minutes. Error on the over-reducing side (you can always add a bit of extra apple cider to the reduced amount). Move the cider reduction to a measuring cup that is heatproof and cool fully, about 30 minutes.

2. In a wide bowl, put 3 cups of all-purpose flour, 1/2 cup of light brown powdered sugar, 1 teaspoon of crushed cinnamon, 1 teaspoon of ground ginger, 2 teaspoons of baking powder, 1/2 teaspoon of kosher salt and 1/2 teaspoon of baking soda to mix.

3. Grate 8 tablespoons of cold unsalted butter on a grater's large holes. Add the grated butter to the flour mixture and melt the butter with your fingers until it is about the size of tiny pebbles. Create a well in the center of the mixture. Add the 1 cup reduced cider and 1/2 cup cold milk to the well and mix the dough using a large spatula.

4. Shaping the dough: Sprinkle a few spoonful's of flour on a work surface. Put the batter on the floor. Pat the dough with a rolling pin into an even layer about 1 inch thick, then add more flour. Fold on the dough and pat it down until 1-inch thick. Again fold and pat, repeat the process six times, until the dough is slightly springy. Pat the dough into a 9x13-inch rough rectangle about 1/2 inches thick.

5. Cut donuts with a floured donut cutter (or 3 inches and 1 inch round cutter) out of the dough. From the first round of cutting, you will be getting around 8 donuts. Place the doughnuts onto a butter paper. Collect the scraps, pat the dough down again and repeat cutting until approximately 18 donuts are in place. Refrigerate the donuts for about 10 minutes, while preheating the air fryer to 375°F.

6. Prepare the coating: Melt and put the remaining 8 tablespoons of butter in a medium dish. In a small bowl, place 1 cup of granulated sugar and 1 teaspoon of ground cinnamon, and whisk with a fork.

7. Cooking: Air fry in groups of 3 to 4 at a time, flipping them halfway through, 12 minutes per group, depending on the size of your air fryer; switch the donuts to a wire rack and load the next batch onto the air fryer. In the meantime, first, dip the fried doughnuts in the butter and then cinnamon sugar. Place the wire rack back in. For dipping, serve the donuts warm or at room temperature with the dipping of hot cider.

Recipe Notes:

Make ahead: You should blend the dough and fold it up the night before. Store in the fridge, tightly wrapped and carry to room temperature for 30 minutes before punching out the donut form and air frying.

Storage: These donuts are best eaten on the day you make them, but the remaining donuts stay well at room temperature for up to 2 days in a tightly sealed jar.

Nutrition:

Per serving, based on 14 servings. (% daily value)

Calories: 318|Fat: 12.4 g (19.1%)| Saturated Fat: 7.7 g (38.4%) |Carbs: 49.1 g (16.4%)| Fiber: 1.1 g (4.3%)| Sugars: 25.8 g| Protein: 3.5 g (6.9%)| Sodium: 173.8 mg (7.2%)

47.   Bread Dough And Amaretto Dessert

Preparation time: 10 minutes

Cooking time: 12 minutes

Servings: 12

Ingredients:

- 1 pound bread dough

- 1 cup of sugar

- ½ cup butter, melted

- 1 cup heavy cream

- 12 oz. chocolate chips

- 2 tbsp amaretto liqueur

Directions:

1. Roll dough, cut into 20 slices, and then cut each piece in halves.

2. Brush dough pieces with butter, sprinkle sugar, place them in your air fryer's basket after you've brushed it some butter, cook them at 350 degrees F for 5 minutes, flip them, cook for 3 minutes more and transfer to a platter.

3. Heat a pan with the heavy cream over medium heat, add chocolate chips and stir until they melt.

4. Add liqueur, stir again, transfer to a bowl and serve bread dippers with this sauce.

5. Enjoy!

Nutrition: calories 200, fat 1, fiber 0, carbs 6, protein 6

48.   Tasty Banana Cake

Preparation time: 10 minutes   Cooking time: 30 minutes

Servings: 4

Ingredients:

- 1 tbsp. butter, soft

- One egg

- 1/3 cup brown sugar

- 2 tbsp. of honey

- One banana, peeled and mashed

- One cup white flour

- 1 tsp. baking powder

- 1/2 teaspoon cinnamon powder

- Cooking spray

Directions:

1. Sprinkle a cooking spray on a cake pan and leave aside.

2. Combine butter and sugar, pineapple, tea, milk, cinnamon, baking powder, and flour in a pot, and whisk

3. Pour this into a spray-filled cake pan, place it in your air fryer and cook for 30 minutes at 350 degrees F.

4. Left the cake to cool, chop and drink.

49.   Pumpkin Pie

Preparation time: 10 minutes

Cooking time: 15 minutes

Servings: 9

Ingredients:

- 1 tbsp. sugar

- 2 tbsp. flour

- 1 tbsp. butter

- 2 tbsp. water

For the pumpkin pie filling:

- 3.5 ounces pumpkin flesh, chopped

- 1 tsp mixed spice

- 1 tsp nutmeg

- 3 oz. water

- One egg whisked

- 1 tsp. sugar

Directions:

1. Put 3 ounces water in a pot, bring to a boil over medium-high heat, add pumpkin, egg, one tablespoon sugar, spice, and

nutmeg, stir, boil for 20 minutes, take off the heat and blend using an immersion blender.

2. In a bowl, mix flour with butter, one tablespoon sugar, and two tablespoons water and knead your dough well.

3. Grease a pie pan that fits your air fryer with butter, press dough into the pan, fill with pumpkin pie filling, place in your air fryer's basket, and cook at 360 degrees F for 15 minutes.

4. Slice and serve warm.

    Enjoy!

Nutrition: calories 200, fat 5, fiber 2, carbs 5, protein 6

CHAPTER 13:

Special Recipe

50.   Honey Duck Breasts

Preparation Time: 10 minutes

Cooking Time: 27 Minutes

Servings: 2

Ingredients

- 1smoked duck breast
- 1tbsp. honey
- 1tsp. tomato paste
- 1tbsp. mustard

- ½ tsp. apple vinegar

Direction

1. Mix tomato paste with honey, vinegar and mustard, whisk well. Add duck breast, toss it to coat move it to air fryer and cook at 370 ° F for 15 minutes.
2. Remove duck breast out from fryer. Add to honey mix, toss and loop back to air fryer then cook at 370°F for 6 minutes more.
3. Divide on plates then serve with side salad.

Nutrition:

Calories: 563 kcal

Protein: 59.68 g

Fat: 26.59 g

Carbohydrates: 19.28 g

Conclusion

A ir Fryer Toaster Oven Cookbook is a perfect fit for you. With this new kitchen miracle, you don't need to switch from appliance to appliance to get various delicious meals. Using a single device, you can roast, toast, Air fry, bake, and cook much more. If you haven't brought this kitchen bliss to home or you have it but haven't been able to use it to its full potential, then this cookbook is a right pick! Now you can toast fresh bread slices in the morning and bake an irresistible chicken for dinner, all just by using Air Fryer Toaster Oven.

CPSIA information can be obtained
at www.ICGtesting.com
Printed in the USA
BVHW081701260221
601199BV00009B/849

9 781801 829595